SUMMARY OF HOLY SPIRIT CURSE BREAKER

Your Supernatural Secret to Removing Generational Strongholds, Sins, and Cycles

DAVID DIGA HERNANDEZ

D DESTINY IMAGE

Copyright 2024–Destiny Image

All rights reserved. This book is protected by the copyright laws of the United States of America. This book may not be copied or reprinted for commercial gain or profit. The use of short quotations or occasional page copying for personal or group study is permitted and encouraged. Permission will be granted upon request. Unless otherwise indicated, all scripture quotations are taken from the *King James Version* of the Bible. Used by permission. All rights reserved.

All emphasis within Scripture quotations is the author's own. Please note that Destiny Image's publishing style capitalizes certain pronouns in Scripture that refer to the Father, Son, and Holy Spirit, and may differ from some publishers' styles. Take note that the name satan and related names are not capitalized. We choose not to acknowledge him, even to the point of violating grammatical rules.

Destiny Image P.O. Box 310, Shippensburg, PA 17257-0310

This book and all other Destiny Image's books are available at Christian bookstores and distributors worldwide.

For Worldwide Distribution.

Reach us on the Internet: www.destinyimage.com.

ISBN 13 TP: 9780768483819

ISBN 13 eBook: 9780768483826

CONTENTS

Introduction	v
1. Blessed or Cursed?	1
2. The Power of a Word Curse	5
3. The Power of a Generational Curse	9
4. Why Do Curses Seem to Work?	13
5. Generational Dysfunction	17
6. Internal Dysfunction	20
7. External Dysfunction	24
8. Holy Spirit: The Curse Breaker	28
About the Publisher	31

INTRODUCTION

❦

Introduction to the Summary of "Holy Spirit: The Curse Breaker"

In "Holy Spirit: The Curse Breaker," the author tackles the profound misconceptions surrounding the idea of curses in the Christian faith, particularly the belief that believers can be under demonic curses due to generational sins or personal hardships. This chapter elucidates the powerful role of the Holy Spirit in liberating believers from the chains of these misconceptions. Through scriptural insights and theological clarity, the author emphasizes that the Holy Spirit, as the indwelling presence of God's truth and grace, debunks the myths of curses and positions the believer in a place of undeniable blessing and divine favor. This summary distills the key themes and messages of the chapter, aiming to reinforce the understanding that with the Holy Spirit, no curse can prevail against God's promises and blessings.

CHAPTER 1

BLESSED OR CURSED?

Bible Verse

"For those who rely on faith are blessed along with Abraham, the man of faith." – Galatians 3:9 (NIV)

Introduction

This chapter explores the profound spiritual heritage and personal journey of the author, who delves into the intense spiritual warfare over his soul, stemming from his ancestral connection to a powerful warlock. The narrative transitions from the author's battles with demonic forces to his transformative encounter with Jesus, emphasizing the biblical concepts of blessing and curse.

Word of Wisdom

"When Jesus walked in, every demon ran out. The torment was gone. The anxiety was gone. All I could do was cry with

relief and gratitude." David Diga Hernandez

Main Theme

The main theme of the chapter revolves around the spiritual legacy of the author's family, the battle between light and darkness, and the ultimate triumph of divine blessing over curses through faith in Jesus Christ.

Key Points

The author's great-great-grandfather was a warlock whose dealings with demonic powers affected generations.

By the age of seven, the author experienced severe depression and anxiety, which he describes as demonic torment.

A pivotal moment occurred during a family Bible conference when the author, overwhelmed by demonic oppression, decided to dedicate his life to Jesus.

This commitment led to a profound spiritual experience where the author felt the love and peace of Jesus, driving away all demonic presence.

The biblical concept of blessing is foundational, starting from God's blessings to Adam and Eve and extending to all who live in faith.

The curse, conversely, originates from disobedience to God's word, as illustrated by the fall of Adam and Eve.

Key Themes

- **Generational Curses and Redemption:** The narrative begins with a recounting of the author's heritage, marked by spiritual darkness due to ancestral choices, setting the stage for his personal struggles and ultimate redemption through faith, illustrating the Christian belief in the power of Jesus to break generational curses.
- **Spiritual Warfare and Deliverance:** The author vividly describes his encounters with demonic entities and the intense spiritual warfare for his soul, highlighting his dramatic deliverance through a personal acceptance of Jesus Christ, which signifies the transformative power of faith and prayer in Christian doctrine.
- **The Power of the Sinner's Prayer:** Despite biblical debates about the format of prayer, the author emphasizes the efficacy of heartfelt prayer in his moment of conversion, which aligns with evangelical Christian practices that value personal commitment to Christ as a turning point in one's spiritual life.
- **Biblical Dichotomy of Blessing and Curse:** Through scriptural references, the chapter delineates the stark contrasts between living under God's blessing versus enduring a curse, using the story of creation and the fall to illustrate these themes, thereby reinforcing the belief that

human actions have spiritual consequences that align with divine will.
- **Divine Justice and Legal Standing in Christ:** The theological discussion extends to the legal metaphor of justification, where the author assures that believers are legally justified through faith in Christ, negating any "legal right" the enemy might claim, thus promoting a sense of security and righteousness bestowed upon believers.

Conclusion

In "Blessed or Cursed?", the author masterfully interweaves personal experiences with theological insights to argue that the believer's life, while challenged by spiritual and worldly trials, is ultimately governed by the divine pronouncement of blessing through faith in Jesus Christ. This chapter affirms that despite the presence of sin and its consequences, those who are in Christ are liberated from curses and positioned in grace, emphasizing a life of spiritual victory and eternal promise.

CHAPTER 2

THE POWER OF A WORD CURSE

Bible Verse
"Bless those who curse you, pray for those who mistreat you." – Luke 6:28 (NIV)

Introduction

This chapter delves into the concept of word curses, exploring whether believers can be cursed by others, including witches, warlocks, or even fellow believers. It discusses the power of God's curse versus human curses, emphasizing the believer's protection under God's blessing.

Word of Wisdom

"A curse is only as powerful as the one who speaks it." David Diga Hernandez

Main Theme

The primary focus of this chapter is the limited power of human-spoken curses compared to divine pronouncements, and the assurance that believers are shielded from curses through their faith and God's protection.

Key Points

- Human curses lack the creative power of God's spoken word.
- Believers are protected from curses; a curse's impact is tied to the belief in its power.
- The Bible illustrates that only curses with divine backing have true potency.
- Negative self-talk and the words of others can influence thoughts and behaviors, but they do not create reality.
- Prophets and apostles in the Bible spoke judgments or blessings only with God's backing.
- The power of our words is significant but does not compare to the creative authority of God.

Key Themes

- **Limitation of Human Curses:** Human-spoken curses lack the capacity to bring about material change without God's endorsement. This limitation reassures believers that curses directed at them by

others have no real power unless God permits their effect.
- **Influence of Belief in Curses:** The chapter discusses how a person's belief in a curse can affect their perception of events, suggesting that fear and acknowledgment of a curse can give it undue power over one's life. Recognizing this can empower individuals to dismiss unfounded fears.
- **Biblical Examples of Divine Curses:** Scriptural accounts show that God's curses are immediate and effective, contrasting with human curses which lack divine authority. This highlights the sovereignty of God's word over human intentions.
- **Role of Faith and Divine Will:** Faith in God's protection and alignment with His will are depicted as shields against curses. The believer's words carry weight when they echo divine intentions, reinforcing the concept that true power resides in spiritual alignment with God.
- **Impact of Words on Reality:** While human words can influence thoughts and emotions, they do not create reality as God's words can. The chapter argues that understanding this helps believers discern between spiritual truth and superstitious fears.

Conclusion

"The Power of a Word Curse" reassures believers that they are secure under God's dominion, immune to the curses of others. It emphasizes the importance of aligning one's speech with God's will and maintaining faith in His protective and authoritative power. This chapter effectively demystifies the concept of curses in the Christian faith, redirecting focus toward the transformative power of blessing and the spiritual authority believers hold through Christ.

CHAPTER 3

THE POWER OF A GENERATIONAL CURSE

Bible Verse

"Submit yourselves, then, to God. Resist the devil, and he will flee from you." – James 4:7 (NIV)

Introduction

This chapter tackles the concept of generational curses, examining biblical perspectives and distinguishing between the myths and realities associated with the idea. It clarifies the nature of curses, the impact of ancestral sins, and the power of personal choice and divine grace for the born-again believer.

Word of Wisdom

"You may have been born into a troubled family, but you were born again into the family of God by the Holy Spirit."
David Diga Hernandez

Main Theme

Exploring the concept of generational curses, this chapter asserts that true spiritual bondage cannot be inherited through family lines among believers, but rather that each individual is responsible for their own spiritual standing before God.

Key Points

- Generational curses, as traditionally understood, are not biblically supported in the context of affecting born-again believers.
- Ancestral sins do not grant demons any legal right over the lives of believers.
- The term 'generational curse' should be replaced with 'generational consequences' to emphasize personal responsibility.
- True freedom from any form of curse is obtained through simple faith and submission to God.
- The believer's new identity in Christ breaks any ties to supposed generational curses.

Key Themes

- **Distinction Between Curses and Consequences:** The chapter clarifies that while generational consequences exist due to the natural effects of sin, there is no spiritual curse carrying over to believers

who are in Christ. This distinction removes the fear associated with generational curses and refocuses on personal responsibility and divine grace.
- **Role of Personal Faith in Overcoming Curses:** It is emphasized that the believer's faith and relationship with God are paramount in overcoming any and all curses. Personal submission to God is the key to breaking any negative patterns that may seem to run in families.
- **Impact of Christ's Sacrifice:** The sacrifice of Christ is presented as the ultimate antidote to any curse, generational or otherwise. The cross of Christ is a pivotal point for believers, marking the end of all curses and the beginning of new life.
- **New Identity in Christ as a Defining Factor:** Once a person becomes a believer, their identity in Christ overshadows any alleged generational curse. This new identity is foundational to understanding and experiencing freedom from curses.
- **Practical Steps to Freedom:** Practical advice is given on how to live free from the influence of generational consequences—through living rightly and in submission to God, rather than through special rituals or uncovering family secrets.

Conclusion

"The Power of a Generational Curse" reassures believers of their complete freedom from the bondage of curses through their new identity in

Christ. By focusing on the transformative power of faith and the significance of personal choices, the chapter empowers readers to reject fear-based teachings on generational curses and embrace the liberating truth of the gospel.

CHAPTER 4

WHY DO CURSES SEEM TO WORK?

Bible Verse

"Put on the full armor of God, so that you can take your stand against the devil's schemes." – Ephesians 6:11 (NIV)

Introduction

This chapter explores why curses seem to affect believers, focusing on the role of deception in amplifying the perceived power of curses and how believers can combat this through spiritual discernment and the armor of God.

Word of Wisdom

"The only way the devil can defeat you is if he can deceive you." David Diga Hernandez

Main Theme

The chapter challenges the effectiveness of curses against believers, emphasizing that any perceived power of curses is actually rooted in deception and a believer's compromise or misunderstanding of spiritual truths.

Key Points

- Believers may experience attacks, but these are not curses; they are tests of faith and moments of spiritual warfare.

- The devil's primary weapon is deception, manipulating believers into fearing more than they need.

- The armor of God is crucial for standing firm against satanic deception.

- Spiritual attacks often manifest as deceptive thoughts that lead to destructive behavior.

- True spiritual victory comes from understanding and living out the truth of God's Word.

Key Themes

- **Deception as the Root of Perceived Curses:** The enemy uses deception to make believers think they are cursed, impacting their emotions and decisions. Understanding this can liberate believers from unnecessary fear and empower them to live in victory.
- **Importance of the Armor of God:** Wearing the full armor of God provides

believers with the tools needed to discern truth from lies, protecting them from the enemy's deceptive tactics. This armor is not just metaphorical but represents daily practices of faith, truth, righteousness, salvation, and the Word of God.

- **Difference Between Attack and Curse:** It's vital to distinguish between being under attack and being cursed. An attack is a moment of temptation or trial that can be overcome, whereas a curse implies unwarranted and continual defeat, which is not theologically sound for a believer.
- **Role of Personal Responsibility in Spiritual Warfare:** Believers are called to actively resist the devil by upholding truth and righteousness. This active resistance is crucial in preventing any foothold of the enemy in their lives.
- **Power of Belief in Spiritual Outcomes:** The chapter argues that a believer's faith significantly influences their spiritual experiences. Believing in the truth of God's protection and promises is more powerful than any curse or negative influence.

Conclusion

"Why Do Curses Seem to Work?" demystifies the concept of curses in the lives of believers by attributing any perceived effects to deception. By equipping themselves with the armor of God and standing firm in their faith, believers can overcome any form of spiritual deception. This chapter calls believers to embrace their authority in Christ, reject fears based on deception, and walk in the victorious reality of their faith.

CHAPTER 5

GENERATIONAL DYSFUNCTION

Bible Verse

"Therefore, if anyone is in Christ, the new creation has come: The old has gone, the new is here!" – 2 Corinthians 5:17 (NIV)

Introduction

This chapter delves into the concept of generational dysfunction, distinguishing it from the often misunderstood notion of generational curses. It emphasizes personal accountability and the power of choice in overcoming inherited challenges.

Word of Wisdom

"Consequences and conditions are not curses." David Diga Hernandez

Main Theme

Generational dysfunction stems from patterns and behaviors passed down through families but does not equate to inescapable curses. Individuals have the power to make different choices and are not doomed to repeat their ancestors' mistakes.

Key Points

- Generational dysfunction is influenced by upbringing, genetics, and family dynamics.
- Conditions created by one's ancestors establish the environment but don't dictate personal destiny.
- Personal responsibility is crucial in overcoming generational challenges.
- Scripture emphasizes that individuals are responsible for their own sins, not those of their ancestors.
- Belief in generational curses can lead to unnecessary fear and a sense of helplessness.

Key Themes

- **Real Effects of Generational Influence:** While generational influences are real and can predispose individuals to certain behaviors, they do not bind individuals to a fate. Each person has the capacity to make choices that diverge from their familial patterns.
- **Scriptural Clarification on Sin and Responsibility:** The Bible clarifies that

while sin has introduced a fallen state into the world, each individual's sin is their own responsibility. This undermines the belief that we are punished for our ancestors' sins and highlights personal accountability.
- **The Role of Personal Choices:** It's our personal choices, not our inherited conditions, that truly shape our lives. Even in the face of adverse inherited conditions, individuals can choose paths that lead to different outcomes, proving the power of personal agency.
- **Psychological and Spiritual Insight:** The chapter bridges psychological understanding and spiritual principles, showing that both realms acknowledge the impact of generational patterns but also affirm the potential for individual change and growth.
- **Empowerment through Faith and Action:** By recognizing the difference between generational consequences and curses, believers are empowered to live out their faith actively, making choices that reflect their new identity in Christ rather than their earthly lineage.

Conclusion

"Generational Dysfunction" refutes the fatalistic notion of generational curses and champions the transformative power of personal choice and divine grace. By embracing their identity as new creations in Christ, individuals can overcome any negative legacies and forge paths marked by faith, righteousness, and personal responsibility.

CHAPTER 6

INTERNAL DYSFUNCTION

Bible Verse

"For the weapons of our warfare are not carnal, but mighty through God to the pulling down of strongholds." – 2 Corinthians 10:4 (KJV)

Introduction

This chapter explores the concept of internal dysfunction, focusing on persistent negative thoughts and emotions that believers may experience, such as anxiety, depression, and intrusive thoughts. It challenges the notion of these struggles being curses and instead attributes them to spiritual strongholds of deception.

Word of Wisdom

"Internal dysfunction is the result of a stronghold, not a curse or a hex." David Diga Hernandez

Main Theme

The battle against internal dysfunction involves recognizing and dismantling mental strongholds built on deception, not merely addressing the symptoms but attacking the root lies that sustain these strongholds.

Key Points

• Believers can experience severe anxiety and depression, but these are not indications of demonic possession or curses.

• Spiritual strongholds in the mind are fortresses of false beliefs that must be torn down.

• The root of internal dysfunction is often a deception that contradicts God's truth.

• Spiritual warfare involves replacing lies with the truth of God's Word.

• Deliverance comes from understanding and applying biblical truth, not through emotional responses or physical actions.

Key Themes

- **Understanding Spiritual Strongholds:** Spiritual strongholds are deceptive mindsets that contradict the knowledge of God and must be combated with the truth. These strongholds form the basis for many of the negative emotions and behaviors that believers experience.

- **Role of the Holy Spirit in Overcoming Strongholds:** The Holy Spirit plays a crucial role in revealing the truths of God's Word, which dismantle the lies at the root of spiritual strongholds. Believers are encouraged to lean on the Spirit for revelation and strength in their mental battles.
- **Practical Steps to Freedom:** To break free from internal dysfunction, believers must actively replace false beliefs with biblical truth. This involves a disciplined approach to studying Scripture and applying its truths to every thought and imagination.
- **The Power of Truth Over Deception:** Victory in spiritual warfare is assured through the application of God's truth against the enemy's lies. Emphasizing the power of the truth helps believers understand that they are not helpless against their mental struggles.
- **Misconceptions About Curses:** The chapter dispels the myth that Christians can be cursed with mental health issues, emphasizing that these challenges stem from spiritual strongholds rather than external curses.

Conclusion

"Internal Dysfunction" empowers believers with the knowledge that their mental and emotional battles are not signs of curses but are challenges that can be overcome through spiritual warfare. By identifying and rejecting lies and fortifying their minds with the truth of God's Word, believers can achieve genuine freedom and peace.

CHAPTER 7

EXTERNAL DYSFUNCTION

Bible Verse

"That ye may be the children of your Father which is in heaven: for he maketh his sun to rise on the evil and on the good, and sendeth rain on the just and on the unjust." – Matthew 5:45 (KJV)

Introduction

This chapter addresses the issue of persistent negative situations in a believer's life, clarifying the distinction between chaos and curses. It argues against the common misconception that believers are cursed because of ongoing troubles.

Word of Wisdom

"Chaos is not a curse. Not every battle is bondage." David Diga Hernandez

Main Theme

External dysfunction, or ongoing negative circumstances, is often mistaken for curses; however, this chapter asserts that such dysfunction is part of the Christian life's trials and not an indication of divine disfavor.

Key Points

• Christians often misinterpret continuous negative circumstances as signs of curses.

• Many struggles are a result of personal choices rather than spiritual curses.

• Trials are inevitable in life, even for the faithful.

• Suffering does not mean God has withdrawn His blessing.

• Believers are encouraged to shift their perspective rather than change their circumstances.

Key Themes

- **Misconceptions of Curses and Chaos:** The chapter emphasizes that not every negative event is a spiritual attack and that believers should not view every difficulty as evidence of being cursed. It suggests that life's natural challenges are often mistaken for supernatural afflictions.
- **Role of Personal Responsibility in Negative Circumstances:** It is

highlighted that personal decisions often lead to negative outcomes. The chapter encourages self-reflection on one's actions and their consequences, promoting accountability rather than attributing every problem to external spiritual causes.
- **Theological Perspective on Suffering:** Scriptural references are used to illustrate that suffering is part of the Christian experience and does not signify abandonment by God. It stresses that Jesus Christ and many biblical figures experienced hardship without being cursed.
- **Maintaining Joy and Perspective in Trials:** The chapter advocates for finding joy and growth opportunities in the midst of trials. It challenges believers to maintain a positive outlook and to recognize God's blessings, even in hard times.
- **Spiritual Victory Through the Holy Spirit:** The enduring joy provided by the Holy Spirit in all circumstances is contrasted with the temporary pleasures of the world. Believers are encouraged to seek joy from their spiritual relationship with God rather than from material conditions.

Conclusion

"External Dysfunction" reassures believers that experiencing ongoing challenges does not mean they are cursed or out of favor with God. By understanding and embracing the biblical perspective on trials and by cultivating a Spirit-led joy, believers can overcome the perception of being cursed and recognize the growth and blessings in their challenges.

CHAPTER 8

HOLY SPIRIT: THE CURSE BREAKER

Bible Verse

Galatians 3:14 (NIV): "He redeemed us in order that the blessing given to Abraham might come to the Gentiles through Christ Jesus, so that by faith we might receive the promise of the Spirit."

Introduction

This chapter discusses the misconceptions about curses among believers, emphasizing that true Christians, guided and inhabited by the Holy Spirit, cannot be cursed. The focus is on the distinction between experiencing life's hardships and being under a curse.

Word of Wisdom

"Conditions don't negate choices."
David Diga Hernandez

SUMMARY OF HOLY SPIRIT CURSE BREAKER

Main Theme

The Holy Spirit is portrayed as the ultimate liberator from the false beliefs in curses, empowering believers to live above the deceptions and accusations of the enemy.

Key Points

- Demons and poor choices can influence, but not curse, a believer's life.

- Believers may repeat past mistakes, but these are consequences, not curses.

- Negative feelings and thoughts can be mistaken for curses but are actually deceptive tactics by the enemy.

- The Holy Spirit is the testament of God's blessing on believers, nullifying any supposed curses.

- True freedom comes from understanding and accepting the Holy Spirit's truth about our blessed status.

Key Themes

- **Misconceptions of Curses:** The enemy uses generational consequences and emotional turmoil to deceive believers into thinking they are cursed. However, these are not indications of curses but rather challenges and trials that all humans face.
- **Role of the Holy Spirit:** The Holy Spirit counters curses and accusations by affirming the believer's righteous standing

before God. This truth breaks the stronghold of any generational or word curses believed by the Christian.
- **Empowerment Against Generational Dysfunction:** Through the Holy Spirit, believers can overcome the repeated dysfunctions of their ancestors by making godly choices that break past patterns.
- **Overcoming Internal and External Dysfunction:** The Holy Spirit helps believers overcome internal deceptions and external hardships by grounding them in spiritual truth and divine joy.
- **Settling the Matter of Curses:** True understanding and freedom from the notion of curses are achieved when believers grasp and embrace the truth imparted by the Holy Spirit—that they are blessed and not cursed, irrespective of circumstances.

Conclusion

The Holy Spirit is the definitive breaker of curses, empowering believers to rise above misconceptions and live in the freedom of God's truth. Through the Spirit, we are reminded that we are not bound by any curses but are blessed and favored by God.

D DESTINY IMAGE

Destiny Image is a prophetic Christian publisher dedicated to empowering believers through Spirit-led messages. Our mission is to equip and inspire individuals to fulfill their God-given destinies by providing transformative resources that resonate with the Charismatic and Pentecostal faith.

We specialize in books, blogs, and back cover copies that reflect prophetic insights, dynamic teachings, and testimonies of faith. Our commitment to fostering spiritual growth and kingdom impact makes Destiny Image a beacon for those seeking to deepen their relationship with God and embrace their calling in the power of the Holy Spirit.